LEARN SCIENCE WITH MO

HUMAN BODY

Paul Mason

Michael Buxton

Published in 2025 by Enslow Publishing, LLC
2544 Clinton Street
Buffalo, NY 14224

First published in Great Britain in 2023 by Wayland

Copyright © Hodder & Stoughton Limited, 2023

Editor: John Hort
Design: Collaborate
Illustrations: Michael Buxton
Science consultant: Peter Riley

All rights reserved. No part of this book may be reproduced in any form without permission in writing from the publisher, except by a reviewer.

Manufactured in the United States of America

CPSIA compliance information: Batch #CSENS25: For further information contact Enslow Publishing LLC, New York, New York at 1-800-398-2504.

Please visit our website, www.enslowpublishing.com. For a free color catalog of all our high-quality books, call toll free 1-800-398-2504 or fax 1-877-980-4454.

Cataloging-in-Publication Data

Names: Mason, Paul, author. | Buxton, Michael, illustrator.
Title: Human body / by Paul Mason, illustrated by Michael Buxton.
Description: Buffalo, NY : Enslow Publishing, 2025. |
Series: Learn science with Mo | Includes glossary.
Identifiers: ISBN 9781978538771 (pbk.) | ISBN 9781978538788 (library bound) |
ISBN 9781978538795 (ebook)
Subjects: LCSH: Human anatomy--Juvenile literature. | Human body--Juvenile literature. |
Human physiology--Juvenile literature.
Classification: LCC QM27.M376 2025 | DDC 612--dc23

Find us on

Contents

Monsters and humans	4
Weight-bearing bones	6
Shot put muscle power	8
Hearing for a fast start	10
Top-shot sight	12
Judo-throw messaging	14
Marathon-swimming breathing	16
Sweaty runners	18
Snack time	20
Fueling road racers	22
Blood around the body	24
Mo picks a sport	26
Mo the wrestler	28
Glossary	30
Books to read / Places to visit	31
Answers	32

The words in **bold** are in the glossary on page 30.

Monsters and HUMANS

Monsters and humans are different (obviously). But monsters are also <u>like</u> humans in lots of ways …

Mo, what things about your body are like a human's?

> **MONSTERS AND HUMANS ARE REALLY LIKE EACH OTHER!**

Inside humans (and monsters) are some important bits you cannot see. For example:

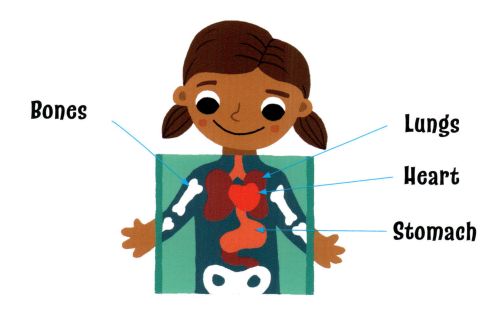

Mo, let's find out more about how humans work. You are going to enjoy this. Let's learn about human bodies by watching them working at their absolute best – at the world's biggest sports contest.

> **THAT DOES SOUND FUN! I COULD MAKE A LIST OF SPORTS TO TRY MYSELF. I'VE ALREADY TRIED CYCLING, BUT MY LEGS DON'T REACH THE PEDALS ...**

Weight-bearing BONES

WE ARE, YES.

Our first sport is weight lifting, which we are watching to find out about bones. You might like this, Mo – you are always saying that monsters are stronger than humans.

In weight lifting, the athlete gets the weight above their head ...

... then holds it there until three white lights go on.

GNNNNN!

COME ... ON ...

Mo, which of these do you think the weight lifter needs most?

a) big feet
b) bones
c) good eyesight
d) an excellent sense of smell

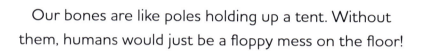

UM ... THE BONES?

Good answer!

All the bones together are called a **skeleton**.

Our bones are like poles holding up a tent. Without them, humans would just be a floppy mess on the floor!

Bones are very strong, but also light. This is because they are made up of different layers:

Hard bone

The outside layer is very strong

Spongy bone

Inside, the bone is a honeycomb shape. It is less strong, but lighter.

Bone marrow

In the middle of the bone is soft bone **marrow**.

Do you know what bone marrow is for, Mo?

UM ...

Bone marrow's most important job is helping to make blood. You can find out about this on pages 24–25.

Shot put
MUSCLE POWER

Next it is time to visit the shot put competition. This will be a good place to find out about **joints** and **muscles**.

Mo, do you know how much the shot put weighs at big competitions?

UM ... NO.

The women's shot put weighs 8.8 pounds (4 kg), about the same as two chihuahuas*. The men's is 16 pounds (7.26 kg).

I hope it's a soft landing.

Wooooo!

* Of course, no one should ever throw any kind of dog.

Without joints and muscles, throwing a shot put would be impossible. In fact, so would moving at all. Let's look at how we throw.

Biceps muscle

Triceps muscle

Elbow joint

When the biceps muscle shortens or **contracts**, the arm bends.

To straighten the arm, the triceps contracts. The bicep lengthens or **relaxes**.

The triceps muscle is important for shot-putters. They throw by opening their arm quickly and with lots of power.

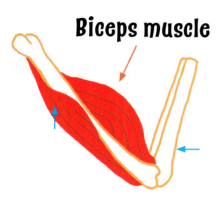

Biceps muscle

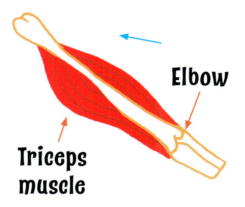

Elbow

Triceps muscle

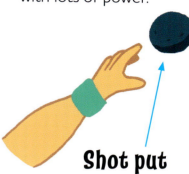

Shot put

Mo, can you think of other jobs where you do the same movement?

 YES I CAN ...

Whack-A-Mole ...

Drumming ...

THERE ARE LOTS!

Those are great examples (unless you are a mole). And that was just ONE joint. There are over 250 joints in the human body.

9

Hearing for a FAST START

Monsters don't like to get wet – so the 50-meter freestyle race is an event you would NOT enjoy, Mo.

NO. WE CAN CROSS THIS ONE OFF MY LIST.

The 50-meter freestyle only lasts about 21 seconds, so a good start is crucial. You must react quickly to the signal. Usually this is a loud "BEEP!"

Let's follow that beep:

1. It starts at a speaker.

2. The speaker makes the air wobble or vibrate.

3. The vibration reaches the swimmer's ear.

> **BUT HOW DOES WOBBLY AIR TELL THE SWIMMER TO DIVE IN?**

Good question, Mo. It happens when the vibration hits the swimmer's ears.

First, the vibrations are funneled inside. The vibration hits a **membrane** called the eardrum.

— Eardrum
— Ear canal

The eardrum starts to **vibrate**. This moves three tiny bones, which happen to be the smallest in a human body.

Hammer — Anvil — Stirrup

The vibration moves to an **organ** called the cochlea, which sends a sound signal to the brain.

Signal line to brain — Cochlea

Hearing is very quick. Less than a second after the beep, the swimmer dives in.

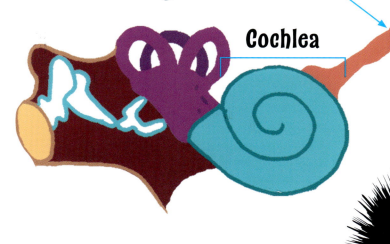

Top-shot SIGHT

Archery competitions are a really good way to see how human (and monster) eyes work. Maybe you could have a try, Mo?

Light travels straight from the target to Mo's eye.

Once the light hits your eye, Mo, it goes into your head. Then your brain turns it into a picture that tells you what is in front of you.

EXCELLENT! HOW DOES THAT HAPPEN, THEN?

How human (and monster) eyes work

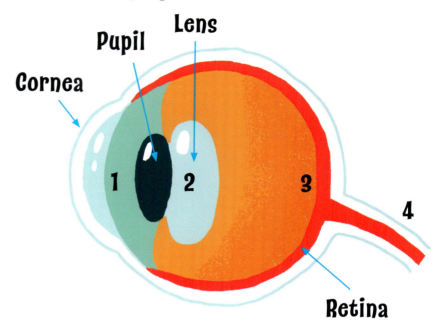

1. Light goes into the eye through the cornea and pupil.

2. Next, the light goes through the lens.

3. The light hits the retina. The retina turns the light into electrical signals.

4. The electrical signals are sent to the brain, which then turns the signals into pictures.

5. Mo lines up the arrow ... then shoots at where the light came from.

QUICK QUIZ

Have you been paying attention? Let's just check, Mo.

When you hear things (like the starting signal on page 10) or see them (like the target on this page), where does the information go?

a) your heart
b) your muscles
c) your brain

Can you help Mo? Find out if you were right on page 32. (And turn the page to find out more about how messages are sent around your body.)

What do you think, Mo — is archery the right sport for you?

JUDO-THROW
messaging

Judo is a sport you might like, Mo. Judo and wrestling are quite similar — and monsters are naturally good at wrestling.

Judo players can win by "throwing" their opponent. Of course, the opponent tries to stop this from happening.

The players feel an attack coming through messages from their **nervous system**.

Whether you are human, monster, or something else, your nervous system carries messages around your body. The nervous system is made up of your brain, spinal cord, and **nerves**.

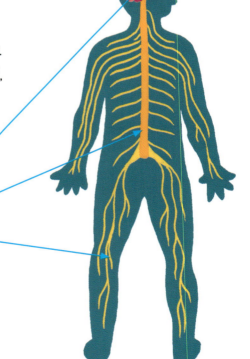

Brain

Spinal cord

Nerves

Mo, try squeezing one hand with the other. Then try squeezing it harder.

The nerves in your hand send different messages when different things happen. The messages travel into your spinal cord, then to your brain. Your brain then works out what to do.

Judo players' nervous systems are very busy during their matches. Messages are zipping all around their bodies!

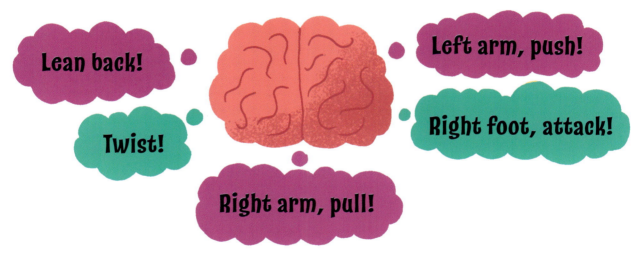

Judo is a battle of the nervous systems, as well as strength and power.

Marathon-swimming BREATHING

Mo, imagine swimming 15.5 miles (25 km). That's what marathon swimmers do at big competitions.

We can do an experiment to learn about this. First, count how many breaths you normally take in 15 seconds.

Now run quickly for 15 seconds. It can be on the spot, in the playground or the park — just not in the road. Afterwards, count your breaths again.

So you took more breaths when your muscles were working hard. This is because there is something in air that your muscles need for energy: oxygen.

The more work muscles do, the more oxygen they need. Oxygen gets into the human body through organs called lungs.

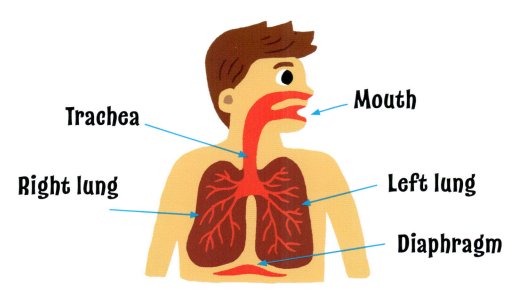

To suck in air, a sheet of muscle called the diaphragm contracts. It pulls the bottom of the lungs downwards, making them bigger. Air is sucked in to fill the extra space.

Diaphragm relaxed

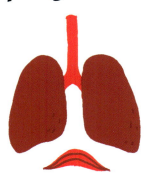

Air pushed out

Diaphragm contracted

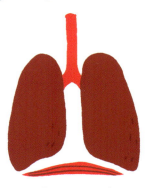

Air sucked in

I DON'T WANT TO DO MARATHON SWIMMING. THANK YOU, THOUGH.

SWEATY runners

Marathon runners have to go even further than marathon swimmers — 26.2 miles (42.2 km), to be exact. That's like running 120 times around a soccer pitch.

THAT'S NOT FOR ME. MONSTERS ARE BUILT FOR STRENGTH, NOT DISTANCE.

Mo, what happened when you did the experiment on page 16? You took extra breaths, but did you notice something else happen as well?

YES! I GOT ALL HOT AND SWEATY.

When we exercise, we get hot. Can you think of some ways this is useful, Mo?

YES – ON A COLD DAY OUTSIDE!

QUICK QUIZ

Let's just check if you understand breathing and sweating.

1 When you breathe more quickly, is it usually because:

    a) you are about to start singing?

    b) your muscles need energy?

    c) you need more air to cool down?

2 Is sweating most often caused by:

    a) your body needing to cool down?

    b) the room you are in being too hot?

    c) each of the above?

OK!

Sometimes, doing a bit of exercise to warm yourself up is useful. But if your body gets TOO hot, it stops working properly.

Sweating is a way for humans (including marathon runners) to keep their bodies cool.

SWEAT

SWEAT

As sweat leaves your skin, it takes away heat.

If you sweat a lot, it is important to replace the liquid you have lost. That is why marathon runners (and swimmers) keep having drinks.

WELL, I AM GOOD AT SWEATING ... BUT I STILL DON'T WANT TO RUN A MARATHON!

SNACK TIME

Mo, has (watching) all this activity made you hungry?

YES. BUT I'M ALWAYS HUNGRY.

That is because you are growing. Like the athletes, your body needs regular supplies of food. Food gives you energy and **nutrients.** These are especially important for young humans (and monsters).

HOW DO CARROTS GIVE ME ENERGY THEN?

We can follow a carrot's journey through a human's **digestive system** to find out.

1. First the carrot gets mashed up by the teeth.

Otherwise it would be impossible to swallow.

CARROTS ARE A GREAT SOURCE OF IMPORTANT VITAMINS AND MINERALS.

2. Next, the carrot is swallowed and travels through the esophagus ...

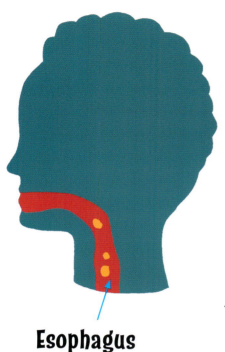

... down into the stomach. It gets turned into a liquid called chyme.

Esophagus

Chyme in here

Small intestine

3. In the small intestine, most of the nutrients and energy are sucked out of the food and into the body.

As the food passes along, water is also sucked out.

4. By the time it reaches the large intestine, the food is changing from liquid to solid.

At the end of the large intestine, most of the energy, nutrients, and water have been taken out.

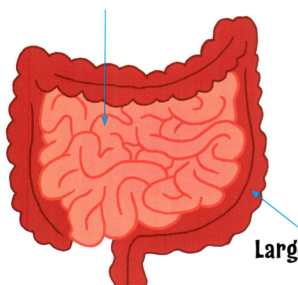

Large intestine

5. What is left is poop!

Poop out here

SO THAT'S HOW POOP IS MADE! EW.

Fueling road RACERS

Mo, would you get hungry if you had to ride a bike for six hours? That is what the road racers do at the biggest races.

THERE WOULDN'T BE ENOUGH FOOD FOR HOW HUNGRY I WOULD BE.

ONLY 159 MILES (256 KM) TO GO!

159 mi to go

To keep going for this long, the racers need to eat and drink. Otherwise they will run out of energy and not be able to keep cycling.

Food and drink quiz

Mo, try this quiz to find out more about food, drink, and exercise. You can find out the answers on page 32. And remember, there might be more than one right answer!

1 WHEN TO EAT?

You are going for a really long walk with Sid. Is it best to eat:

a) A small meal 1–2 hours before the walk?

b) Little snacks as you go along?

c) When you get back (after all, by then you will be REALLY hungry)?

2 WHAT TO EAT?

What kind of food makes the best snacks for your hike?

a) Chocolate and potato chips

b) a small sandwich

3 WHEN TO DRINK?

You are going to play soccer for 40 minutes. Should you drink before you play?

a) Yes, as much as I can.

b) Yes, but just a glass will be enough.

c) No, I don't want water sloshing around inside me while I'm playing soccer.

ALL OF THEM! HAHA!

I JUST DRINK WHEN I'M THIRSTY!

Feeling thirsty is your body telling you it is running out of water. It would have been better to drink before that. A glass of water 30 minutes before and little drinks all through the game would have been best.

BLOOD
around the body

Mo, when we were watching the cyclists, did you see that they all had little computers on their handlebars?

YES. ARE THEY WATCHING TV BECAUSE THE RACE IS SO LONG AND BORING?

No! The computer is telling them:

- Time riding
- Power
- Distance
- Speed
- BPM (heartbeats per minute)
- Pedaling speed

The most important number is the rider's **BPM.** This measures how quickly the heart pumps blood around the body.

The heart is a pump made of muscle. Its four chambers contract and relax to squirt blood around the body.

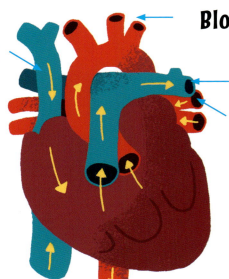

Blood in from body

Blood out to body

Blood out to lungs

Blood in from lung

Blood is the body's delivery service. It takes oxygen and nutrients to where they are needed. It also removes waste.

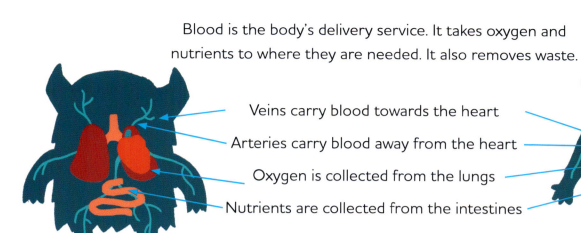

- Veins carry blood towards the heart
- Arteries carry blood away from the heart
- Oxygen is collected from the lungs
- Nutrients are collected from the intestines

HUMANS AND MONSTERS ARE PRACTICALLY THE SAME UNDER THE SKIN!

Mo, what do you think happens to the cyclists' heartbeats per minute when they start to go faster?

WELL ...
THEIR BODIES NEED MORE OXYGEN AND NUTRIENTS, SO ...
IT MUST GO UP!

Correct! Now, would you like some cycle training?

NOOOO.

MO PICKS
a sport

Mo, there is one more subject to explore before you decide which sport to take up. It has a great name for impressing your friends: somatotyping.

TOMATO TYPING?

Almost. Somatotypes are body shapes. The three extremes are endomorph, ectomorph, and mesomorph. Each body shape has different things it is often especially good at.

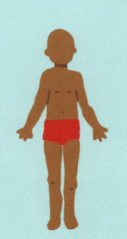

Ectomorph

Ectomorphs are light with small muscles. They are often good at endurance sports, which go on for a long time. For example:

Racewalking

Marathon running

Basketball

Soccer

Sumo wrestling

Weight lifting

Shot put, discus, and hammer throwing

Football lineman

Wrestling

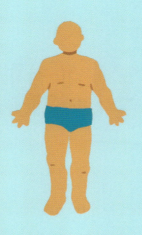

Endomorph

With a wider shape, endomorphs have large muscles. They are often good at sports that need lots of strength and power. You can see examples of these to the left.

Mesomorph

With wide shoulders and narrow hips, mesomorphs are often good at sports that need speed and power. For example:

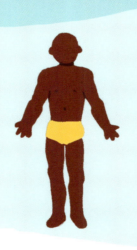

Any sprinting sport

Swimming

Gymnastics

Triathlon

Combat sports

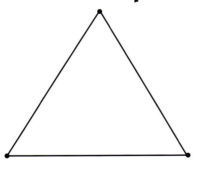

Almost no one is a pure ectomorph, endomorph, or mesomorph. Most humans fit somewhere in between.

Whatever shape you are, there are plenty of sports that will suit you. So, Mo, which one are you going to pick?

EASY! I'M GOING TO BE A ... WRESTLER!

27

Mo THE WRESTLER

Now that Mo has decided to become a top wrestler, Mo's coach has written a plan for how to achieve this.

Monsters are naturally good at wrestling, but the plan also includes ways to get fitter and healthier.

Mo's plan for getting stronger and fitter:

FITNESS TRAINING

Monday: long walk (at least 3 miles [5 km]) or bike ride (at least 18 miles [30 km]).

I'LL GO FOR THE WALK – NOT THE BIKE RIDE!

Tuesday: wrestling practice at gym

Wednesday: rest day

Thursday: rest day/other sports

Friday: wrestling practice at gym

Saturday: rest day/competitions/other sports

Sunday: strength training

STRENGTH TRAINING

High-stepping on the spot for 20 steps, while windmilling arms

Heel flicks for 20 steps

10 squats

3 x plank for 10 seconds

5 x tricep dips

5 x glute bridges, held for 5 seconds

> PHEW!
> THAT LOOKS LIKE A LOT OF WORK ...
> IT'S A GOOD THING I LOVE WRESTLING!

FOOD FOR TRAINING

Normal meals, plus:

2 hours before training, a sandwich or small bowl of rice/pasta for energy

30 minutes before training: drink 16 ounces (500 ml) of water (and more while training, too).

ZZZZZ ZZZZZ ZZZZZ

Sleep helps your body recover. Top athletes sometimes have a nap in the afternoon, to get a bit of extra sleep.

Glossary

BPM
short for Beats Per Minute, telling you how fast or slow someone's heart is beating

contract
to get smaller

digest
to break down food, then take the useful part of it into the body

digestive system
parts of the body that help digest food. In humans, the main parts are the mouth, stomach, and intestines.

discus
a heavy, circular, platelike object. In sports contests, the aim is to throw the discus as far as possible.

hammer throw
a sports contest with the aim of throwing a 'hammer" (a heavy weight at the end of a chain) as far as possible

joint
a place where two bones are joined together. Knees, elbows, shoulders, and knuckles are all joints.

marrow
the soft material in the middle of a bone

membrane
a thin skin or layer of material

muscle
material inside the body that is able to contract and relax, helping the body to move

nerves
parts of the nervous system that send signals to the brain (for example: "You are touching something hot.") and get signals back ("Take your hand away!')

nervous system
the messaging service that carries signals to and from the brain

nutrient
something the body needs to help it survive, grow, and stay healthy

organ
a part of the body that has a special job to do. For example, the heart is an organ and its job is to pump blood.

relax
to become softer and looser (when muscles relax, they usually get longer)

skeleton
all the bones that give a body its basic shape

vibrate
to wobble or shake in a rhythmic way

Books to read

Quick Fix Science: The Human Body by Paul Mason (Wayland, 2021)
Meet Snappy, a young Nile crocodile. Snappy is really interested in science, but not all that good at it — yet. Somehow Snappy already knows quite a bit about human bodies, but in this book he finds out more.

Disgusting and Dreadful Science: Smelly Farts and other Body Horrors by Anna Claybourne (Franklin Watts, 2021). Snot, sweat, foot fungus, diarrhea, and more — if it's revolting and linked to the human body, you will find scientific information about it here.

Body Bits: Hair-raising Human Body Facts by Paul Mason and Dave Smith (Wayland, 2020)
Leaning towards the horrifying and humorous, this book features fascinating facts and funny cartoons. It is part of the "Body Bits" series, which also has books on plant parts, animal parts, and dinosaur body bits.

Places to visit

The Mütter Museum

19 S. 22nd Street
Philadelphia, PA 19103

This museum's displays help visitors better understand the mysteries of the human body and appreciate the fascinating history of medicine.

The Health Museum
John P. McGovern Museum of Health and Medical Science

1515 Herman Drive
Houston, TX 77004

This museum features a larger-than-life model of the human body that visitors can actually walk through! Interactive audio and video stations encourage visitors to ask their top questions about the human body and the history of medical science.

Answers

Page 13

c) is correct. The messages go to your brain. The brain then works out what the signals from your ears and eyes mean, then decides what you should do about them.

Page 19

1 b) is correct. To get energy, your muscles need oxygen, which comes from your lungs. The more energy your muscles need, the more the lungs breathe in and out.

2 c) is correct. Your body sweats when it needs to cool down. This could be because it has gotten too hot because you are working hard and getting hot, or because the room you are in is too hot.

Page 23

Question 1: Mo was right! a), b), and c) are all correct.

Eating before lets your body digest the food, storing energy. Small snacks will keep up your energy. And later, the right food will help your body recover.

Question 2: b) is the best answer. Chocolate and potato chips would give you a quick burst of energy, but it does not last for long. A sandwich would give long-lasting energy to keep you going.

Question 3: b) is the right answer. A glass of water 30 minutes before the game (and little drinks all through it) is the best way to give your body the water it needs. Feeling thirsty is your body telling you it is running out of water, so it is best to drink before that.